Coping with the Wobbles of Life

Doreen Harrison

WIPF & STOCK · Eugene, Oregon

Wipf and Stock Publishers
199 W 8th Ave, Suite 3
Eugene, OR 97401

Coping With the Wobbles of Life
By Harrison, Doreen
Copyright©2016 Apostolos
ISBN 13: 978-1-5326-6942-2
Publication date 9/23/2018
Previously published by Apostolos, 2016

Contents

Coping with the Wobbles of Life 6

Weather 9

The Singer 12

Love 15

Accepted 18

Take Time to Listen 21

God's Name 24

Incredible 27

God's Plans 30

God is our Refuge 33

A Modern Psalm 36

Dandelions 38

Silence is Golden 42

In the Right Position 45

Replay 48

Stall 51

Chorus Line of Heavenly Sunbeams 54

Wols 57

Coping with the Wobbles of Life

Most families have particular traditions associated with birthdays. In our family, a birthday tea is not complete without jelly as dessert. Recently, we celebrated a birthday in Bristol and we were sent on our home ward journey with a glass bowl, full of very wobbly jelly, balanced on my lap, in the front seat. Possessed with a vivid imagination, I identified the havoc which an emergency stop could cause!

Often our journey through life has similar problems. We balance a multitude of sloppy situations in our everyday living and if circumstance brings our progress to a sudden halt chaos can ensue. Modern society can be so complicated and unpredictable. Reconsidering the jelly fraught journey, however, I realised that if I had used my common sense, and transferred the jelly to a plastic container with a secure lid, my journey could have had a roller coaster progress without a jelly produced disaster.

So in life, if we trust each day into the care and protection of God, we reach the end of the day with peace in our hearts. This is not just a pious platitude; it is an actual fact of living in faith.

One birthday had been a great success, ending with a crowd of small boys rushing out of the gate chasing a football which bounced into the road just as a car speeded towards them, but they all stopped on the edge of the pavement. No one saw any angel traffic police holding them back, but I am sure they were there.

I remembered this event on the jelly evening when our eldest granddaughter almost stepped out into the path of a car, but, again, stopped just in time. God gave us common sense, along with His other gifts. Common sense should make us aware of His presence and power and remind us to live each day with the song of faith, described in Psalm 89. *"I will sing of the Lord's unfailing love for ever. Your faithfulness is as enduring as the heavens."*

Weather

One topic of conversation which never fails is the weather. An unforgettable spell of amazing weather will provide conversation for years after it has occurred; is this one reason why the story of Noah's Ark is so well known? I noted these items of weather below and also affirm their accuracy!

"A sun-shiny shower won't last half an hour."

"If the moon rises with a halo round, soon we'll tread on deluged ground."

"Clear moon, frost soon."

One I shall keep in mind until next August is this:

"If the sun shines through the apple trees upon a Christmas day, when Autumn comes they will a load of fruit display."

The 1933 Education syllabus contained this advice in the section headed, 'Holding the children's interest':

"When all else fails, direct the pupils attention to the ever changing panoply of the sky."

Our Welsh poet R Thomas captured the same thought. "In Wales there are jewels to gather, but with the eye only. A hill lights up suddenly, a field trembles with colour and goes out in its turn. In one day you can witness the extent of the spectrum."

The weather embodies all the colours of the rainbow! When Noah and his family came out of the Ark, God set the first rainbow in the sky. He said, "I have placed my rainbow in the clouds. It is the sign of my covenant with you and with all the earth." This weather sign is absolutely trustworthy.

Keep in mind the message of the rainbow, which represents God's covenant of love and mercy. Enjoy a happy and blessed year whatever the weather! God is still in control.

The Singer

There was a man whose ambition was to serve God, and so he entered a monastery. Here the monks spent time in prayer and praise and he had space and time to honour God as he wanted to do. However, when they met together for praise and worship there was a problem. He was tone deaf and his singing produced a discord of such concern that eventually the Choir Master suggested that he mimed to the music and just sang with his heart and mind!

One night, he had a dream. It was Evensong and all the monks were assembled in the chapel. They were singing and he saw himself amongst them, miming the words.

One voice rose above the rest with such harmony and power that, one by one, the other monks stopped singing to listen. Finally, the only singer was the owner of the majestic voice and he saw, to his amazement, that he was that singer!

Then he saw Jesus standing beside him. Jesus smiled and said, "Brother, always remember this. I hear the singer, not the song."

To attend church each Sunday, to belong to a choir, to give money to charities, these are good things to do, but their performance does not make us a Christian. A true Christian has undergone a change of heart, which the Bible describes as a New Birth.

Psalm 40 puts it like this:

"The Lord turned to me and heard my cry. He lifted me out of the pit of despair, out of the mud and the mire. He set my feet on solid ground and steadied me as I walked along. God has given me a new song to sing, a hymn of praise to our God. Many will see what He

has done and be amazed. They will put their trust in the Lord."

The Singer matters more than the song.

Love

When there is a disaster of the immensity of an earthquake or a tsunami there is comfort to everyone concerned because of the united desire to alleviate the suffering. There can be a world-wide response to appeals for help. Nation does not rise up against nation and refuse to help because this happened to people of a different colour, class and creed. The heart of the entire world is moved with compassion. The Christian ethic describes this as "Loving your neighbour as you love yourself."

There is a book in the Bible which captures the uncertainty of life on earth. In Job we read that *"Man is born to trouble as surely as the sparks fly upward."* The hero, Job, was bereaved of his ten children, all his flocks and herds and thus his livelihood, and then he was afflicted with such an appalling skin disease that when his friends met up with him "they could hardly recognise him!"

His wife told him, *"Curse God and die!"* Job, who was sitting among the ashes, scraping himself with a piece of broken pottery replied, *"You are talking like a foolish woman. Shall we accept good from God and not trouble?"*

Real love is unconditional. When we accept everyone as a neighbour we are exercising unconditional love. To be able to react to all sorts and conditions of people in this way we need to accept that God's love is unconditional.

Job is recorded as saying, *"Though He slay me, yet will I trust Him."*

Natural disasters occur and questions arise; this is a human response. Chaos can only happen if we allow acts of Nature to depose

God from his position of ultimate responsibility for planet Earth.

Accepted

Friends of ours have a son called Samuel, who has Downs Syndrome. We received a letter from them, with a recent photo. Samuel is in a toy car, at playgroup, laughing at the camera, and obviously enjoying himself. He begins school in September, and there will be adequate care and provision of a class room assistant for him. They describe him as "A happy boy, and everyone loves him."

I was reminded of a true story, concerning another boy with Downs Syndrome. It was sports day at his school and he was determined to run in the races with his classmates. They all lined up, the race began and he tripped and fell. At once, all the other runners stopped, and waited until he got up. Then they all joined hands and, together, crossed the line. One child explained,

"He can't run like we can, but we wanted him to feel part of the race so we decided to run together."

Samuel is happy because he is accepted and appreciated, just as he is. The boy in the race was accepted as part of the group and it was the intention of the group to accommodate to his particular needs. It would be a colourless world if we were all alike, if humanity was just a collection of clones. Society is delightful because of the differences between people and places, the problems begin when one section of society feels superior to another.

The Bible tells us to love our neighbour as we love ourselves. The way to do this is to love the Lord our God with all our heart, soul, mind and strength! Then we are looking at life through the filter of eternity's values and we can agree with the comment which God made, when He first created the earth and all that is in it. He said, "This is good, very good."

We should care that Samuel, and all other children like him, and all other children everywhere, feel accepted and valued as they run the race of life.

Take Time to Listen

I taught a boy called Harry who found everything difficult but who never gave up trying to improve. One morning he produced a page of neat copy writing, and to encourage him I suggested he showed his book to the head teacher.

"Be sure to say that I am very pleased with you," I told him. He set off eagerly, but when he came back, his joy had gone. "He wasn't pleased," he said. "He didn't listen to me, and he didn't like my work."

When I asked the head teacher what had happened, I discovered that when Harry presented his exercise book, it was open at page one. Looking at that page, he certainly did not merit any praise!

"Didn't Harry tell you how much his work had improved?" I asked. The head teacher replied, "I didn't listen!"

I questioned Harry. "Why did you show him your poor work on page one instead of this morning's good work?" Harry looked surprised. "I thought you wanted him to see how much I had improved," he replied. "Well, he needed to see page one if he was going to know how much better my work is now."

This anecdote reminds me of some good advice in the Bible. In the book written by James we read this:

"Everyone should be quick to listen, slow to speak and slow to become angry."

To listen is a courteous act. It allows someone else to present an opinion. It gives someone else centre stage place in a discussion. When we take time to listen to what is actually being said instead of jumping to a conclusion, we will be slow to become angry because we are not reacting on impulse.

Consider this poem written by Will Carleton:

Boys flying kites haul in their white winged birds,

You can't do that way when you're flying words.

Careful with fire is good advice we know,

Careful with words is ten times doubly so.

Thoughts unexpressed may sometimes fall back dead.

But God himself can't kill them when they're said.

God's Name

I heard a story the other day about a man who died and stood before the pearly gates. St Peter greeted him and then said, "In order to come in, you must answer three questions.

"First question, Name two days in the week which begin with the letter T."

The man thought for a short while, and then replied, "Today and tomorrow."

"Second question," said St Peter. "How many seconds in a year?"

"There are twelve," came the reply. "January 2nd, February 2nd, March 2nd ..."

"Right!" said St Peter. "Here is my final question. What is God's first name?"

The man smiled. "I have known His name for a long time," he said. "It's Andy."

"How do you know that?" asked Peter?

"I learned it many years ago, in Sunday school," came the reply. "We used to sing a chorus about his name."

And He (Andy) walks with me, And He (Andy) talks with me, And He tells me I am his own,

And the joys we share as we tarry there, None other has ever known.

When I stand before the pearly gates, there is only one question which I will need to answer. The question will be "Why do I think I can enter heaven?" and the correct answer is "Jesus paid the entrance fee when he died for my sins on the cross. He has promised to reserve a place for me in Heaven. "

As for God's name, because I have put my trust in Jesus, He does walk and talk with me, and one of His gifts is joy. My faith is indeed a living, bright reality...

How about you?

Incredible

Recently I was given a series of explanations about the origins of certain well known sayings. They all seem very plausible.

Some of you who read this will remember a time when a tin bath hung outside the kitchen door. This provided part of the ensuite arrangement for the family. The other part was also outside, in a hut at the bottom of the garden.

When it was bath night, the men of the house used the water first, while it was hot and clean. Then the boys had their turn, followed by the women and the girls. By this time, the water was so dirty, that you could lose someone in it. Baby had the last bath, hence the saying, "Don't throw the baby out with the bath water!"

There was a time when the end of a week of heavy work was celebrated by heavy drinking. Often the man would be unable to reach home and would fall into a ditch to sleep it off. Anyone finding him would carry him home, lay him on the kitchen table and the family would sit around, waiting to see if he was going to wake up. Hence the custom of holding a "Wake".

In those distant days, in case a person was buried when they were not dead but only in a coma, a string could be tied to the wrist of the body to be buried, and the string would lead through the coffin lid and be fixed to a bell.

A watcher would sit in the grave yard to listen for the bell, thus someone could be "saved by the bell," or was considered to be "a dead ringer."

Now, how much of this is true? What sounds credible might actually be incredible! We are regarding these things in the past from the vantage point of the present.

In the generation when these situations occurred, people had a hearty respect for God. The Bible was a well-respected book. Texts were hung on the wall as a reminder of the oversight and protection of the Lord God Almighty. It is incredible that God, the creator of all things, the Lord of Lords, should give attention to the needs and prayers of people like you and me. It is completely true, it is a credible fact, that God so loves this world, that he sent his only son Jesus, that whoever trusts in him will one day move from time into eternity.

Jesus is the same yesterday, today and forever, and Gods love is new every morning.

God's Plans

The missionary nurse was on her way home to the isolated village where she had opened a small clinic. She was accompanied by a native woman who had converted to Christianity, and together they were anticipating a hot meal and a night's rest. As if in answer to prayer, along came a bus. It stopped and the miles sped by. When they reached the place where the track turned up the mountain towards their own village, the missionary went to the front of the bus to ask the driver to let them off.

He refused! "There isn't a bus stop here," he told her.

The bus sped on until, many miles down the road they reached a legitimate bus stop. They were now further away from home than when they had got on the bus.

Then they heard someone calling them. "Is that the nurse?" Turning, they saw a woman approaching, carrying a baby in her arms. "I knew you would be here," she said. "I saw you in my dream." She handed the baby to the missionary, the child was very sick and obviously needed medical care. "I saw, in a dream, that if I came down the mountain and waited just here, a nurse would arrive to help my baby," the mother explained.

The nurse was able to help; she had the required medicines and treatment with her. Having been led to an appointment obviously prepared by God, the long walk home was less arduous than expected.

What a combination of coincidences, you might be thinking. A busy day, an unexpected bus, a surly driver who refused to stop at the requested place. What about a loving God who arranged events so that a sick child could have the help required?

When things do not work out as we want them to do, it is so easy to complain and argue. The Bible reminds us, *"We know that in all things God works for the good of those who love him, who have been called according to his purposes."* His appointment can never be a disappointment.

God is our Refuge

Politicians may pontificate, councillors may conjecture, legislators may present new laws but the fact remains, people need work and there are no jobs available. It is the simple truth, supply does not meet demand. For young people, who have worked for degrees and diplomas, and who are now redundant, the future must seem very bleak. For young people who did not take the opportunity, nor have the inclination, to study for extra qualifications, life has already been bleak for several years.

For older people, whose job situation was curtailed when firms went bankrupt and early retirement was theirs without choice, there is no light on the horizon. Social hand-outs do not include a feeling of self-worth.

My daughter helps out at a Food Bank centre in Bristol. Families who are suddenly without income can apply for food for the next week. She is astounded by the people who are plunged into desperate need because they are no longer employed. State subsidies take time to come through.

The other week, there was an unusual donation of bottles of bubble bath and she included one in a box for a family with young children, along with Kit Kat bars for each child. The mother, with tears in her eyes, said, "Thank you so much. It is a long time since I could include something like this in my weekly shop."

Most of us take bubble bath, scented soap, a vase of flowers, chocolate, as justifiable extras. Some people can no longer risk spending inadequate income on such items. In the "affluent West", we are beginning to feel the pinch of poverty. How do we handle this rising uncertainty? There is a Psalm in the Bible which begins with these words, *"God is our refuge and strength, always ready to help in time of trouble. So, we will not fear."*

When everything and everyone lets you down, you can depend on the kindness of God. He will never fail to meet your need.

A Modern Psalm

See how the sky embraces the mountains,
Cuddles them close in a mantle of mist.

Note how the rain folds a veil of grey lengthways,

Taking their colour and blooming them over,

Like plums ripe for harvest or grapes full of juice.

Sometimes the sun turns them golden in splendour,

As if he arose fresh each day from their heart.

Autumnal glory of bronze, copper, ochre,

Bracken brown, cinnamon, covering contours.

Winter, outlining their beauty in white.

Deep satisfaction there is to live near them

Always such loveliness round us in Wales!

Now these great mountains stand over a valley

With chapel pews empty and temples forsaken.

Times may have changed - but faith stands forever.

These Mountains show us in their silent splendour:

The power and the glory and goodness of God.

Even the winter of our discontent,

Is lightened and brightened by promise of grace.

Sheep still appreciate shelter of mountains.

The Lord is my Shepherd, and I shall not want.

Dandelions

They are everywhere, and they look beautiful.

Dandelions have sprung up throughout the country, three weeks early and in great profusion on account of the unusually warm Spring. There are thousands of them, in lawns, parks, roadsides, meadows and gardens. When the flower heads turn into fluffy clocks, the number of these yellow flowers could increase to many thousands.

Possibly, in a different setting, they would receive the same acclaim as Wordsworth gave to the daffodil. The reason for the increase in these flowers might be the result of added nitrates in soil from cars, industry and fertilisers. Dandelions are rich in nectar which is important for bees and other insects. We are so used to rain enriched country side, so green and flower full, that we are inclined to take it for granted.

To many people, life in a concrete jungle could raise a profusion of dandelions to the status of orchids. Once, Wales was full of chapels and churches. The warmth of faith in years of spiritual revival produced a multitude of opportunities to meet together and praise God for all His goodness to them. There are still church services every Sunday and we have freedom to express our belief in a God who so loved the world that He sent His only Son Jesus to identify with us and, by His death on a cross, to redeem humanity.

However, Easter for many people majors on Easter eggs and Bank holiday celebrations and the glory of the Resurrection truth is ignored. If the situation in society began to deteriorate, would people begin to renew their faith in a God who cares for us? Do we take our present securities for granted? If weed killers removed the brightness of dandelions from our spring landscapes, would we wish we had appreciated their beauty while we still had it to enjoy? In the same way, do we take for granted God's patience and grace? Are we anxious that the sweetness of faith continues to be available in our country?

Silence is Golden

There was an old priest named Zechariah, who had an encounter with an angel.

The angel told him that God had heard his prayers and his wife was going to bear a son. They were both well on in years, and this information seemed so unlikely that Zechariah questioned the angel. *"How can I be sure of this?"* he asked. The angelic reply was unexpected. *"Now you will be silent and unable to speak until the day this happens!"*

I recollect a similar sentence of silence when Joshua was setting out to capture the city of Jericho. The Bible reports Joshua's words, *"Do not give a war cry, do not raise your voices, do not say a word until the day I tell you to shout!"* We human beings can be so quick to speak, to pass an opinion, to embellish an event, to judge, to criticise, to make sure that we have a hearing.

One motto which is vastly under used is the one which reminds us "Silence is golden." In Zechariah's case, silence protected his dear wife, Elizabeth. No one could challenge as unlikely the story that an angel had announced her pregnancy when Zechariah couldn't speak. Gossip was averted, scandal was suppressed, and the dignity of Divine intervention was maintained. In the conquest of Jericho, nobody on the seven day march was allowed to speak doubt, express fear, demoralise anyone else by refuting Joshua's orders and thus diminishing the purpose of God.

In the Bible book written by James, who was Jesus brother, there are these words: *"Take note of this. Everyone should be quick to listen, slow to speak and slow to become angry."* A Proverb states, *"When words are many, sin is not absent, but he who holds his tongue is wise."* We advise our children, "Think before you speak."

Another Proverb affirms, *"The tongue of the righteous is as choice silver."* We should value the gift of speech and use it with care.

In the Right Position

Exactly one year ago, someone gave me a cyclamen plant, bought from a well-known supermarket, and full of graceful, deep pink flowers. It is still in bloom, and I am quite amazed by this. Previous cyclamen have not flourished and I have often called them "sickly men" on account of my inability to keep them bright and beautiful.

So what is different about this one? This time I have identified the correct position in which a cyclamen will flourish in my house and I have kept it in that place! What a simple solution. Last week someone else gave me a lovely cyclamen, and now the particular window sill holds two delightful plants.

Our society is sick! Crisis follows crisis. Families are facing financial problems, students are anticipating huge debts, elderly people are in need of reassurance that there will be compassion and care for their closing years and the Bank of England prints more money in an attempt to fill the gap between cost and cash. We are no longer in the right position!

Schools, Councils and Parliament used to begin each day with prayer. n hospitals ward sisters could pray in the ward, and share a reading from the Bible. Sunday was a day when work stopped and worship was important. The light of the knowledge of the glory of God, in the face of Jesus Christ, made society bright with hope and beautiful with concern. Without central heating; double glazing, and cavity wall insulation we had warm hearts.

I am reminded of a crisis situation described in the Bible, when the people cried out in despair, *"O our God, we do not know what to do but our eyes are on you!"*

The answer came in these words, *"Do not be afraid or discouraged by this vast army, for the battle is not yours, but God's."*

Are we in a position to identify with His help?

Rest Day

I noticed a poster outside a local church which read like this: "7 days' work makes one weak." The way in which weak is spelled contains the punch line of the poster. The human frame was designed with the safety clause of one day in seven as a rest day. Six days of work with one day of rest makes one week!

The Bible identifies this. In the story of creation, by the seventh day, God had finished the work he had been doing, so on the seventh day, he rested from all his work. If the Creator God needs one day in seven as a rest day, so do we.

To introduce the concept of a rest day into the busy schedule of Christmas might seem impossible to achieve. There are cards to write and to post. There are presents to buy and to wrap. There is food to prepare, fridges to fill; it is not only the turkey that gets stuffed at Christmas.

There are people to meet, places to visit. There are memories to contend with. Christmas is crowded with memories. Some are nostalgic, all about Noel as it used to be. Some are very nice and some are nerve wracking. But the overall impression of Christmas is all about doing things, being busy, busy, busy.

The reason for the season gets lost in the hustle and bustle. Surely Christmas is about that peace of God, which passes all understanding. Angels burst through time and sang the reason for the season to a group of startled shepherds in the fields near Bethlehem.

St Luke retells the event. *"The angel said, today, in the town of David, a Saviour has been born. He is Christ the Lord. Suddenly a great company of the heavenly host appeared with the angel, praising God and saying, Glory to God in the highest, and on earth, peace to men on whom his favour rests."*

Whatever is happening around you, the promise of God is that you can know an inner peace which no one can take from you. Make a space, and take time this Christmas, to be still and know God.

Stars

In the story of Christmas, the three wise men feature regularly. They were Magi, scientists, philosophers, astrologers. They identified patterns in the skies and a new pattern would provoke immediate attention. They followed a star to Bethlehem. There were three possible star phenomena at the time of Jesus birth.

In 11 BC Halley's Comet was shooting brilliantly across the skies. In 7 BC there was a brilliant conjunction of Saturn and Jupiter. From 5 BC to 2 BC, Sirius, the Dog Star, rose at sunrise and shone with extraordinary brilliance.

Having arrived in Jerusalem, which was a wise choice as this was the capital city, the wise men inquired at the royal palace, *"Where is He who has been born King of the Jews?"*

Now, the Roman authorities had appointed Herod to be Governor of Palestine in 47 BC, and in 40 BC he received the title of "King" as a reward for services rendered. He died in 4 BC. He had a reputation for immediate suppression of any opposition and when he heard the Wise Men's question he decided to remove this rival for his title as soon as he could.

So he put into action the plan that all babies under the age of two years were to be killed. The Wise Men did not tell Herod where Jesus was, instead they went home by another route. Joseph, warned in a dream, took Mary and Jesus and escaped into Egypt.

There is a delightful legend concerning their escape. On the journey they sheltered for the night in a cave. It was cold, frost covered the ground and a spider spun a web across the entrance to the shelter, which sparkled in the early morning light, as if it was spangled with diamonds.

Along the road came Herod's soldiers, searching for babies. They stopped beside the cave, but their officer said, "Look at the spiders webs intact, there's no one inside that cave." The soldiers moved on and Joseph led his family into safety. That, so it is said, is why we decorate the Christmas tree with tinsel. Stars, tinsel, even a stray spider, let them remind you that God's plans always work out.

Chorus Line of Heavenly Sunbeams

When I was growing up in the industrial North of England, little girls had two ambitions. The first was to be chosen for the chorus line of small sunbeams in the Christmas pantomime at the Alhambra Theatre, Bradford, and the second was to sing in the Huddersfield Choral society. I never achieved either of these ambitions!

However, I have been in the chorus line of Heavenly Sunbeams for 50 years now, and one day I will be part of a choir which exceeds, in size and quality, any human choir ever assembled. This choir is described in the Bible with these words.

"I heard every creature in heaven and on earth and under the earth and on the sea and all that is in them singing, To him who sits on the throne and to the Lamb, be praise and

honour and glory and power for ever and ever."

I became a Christian when I was at teacher training college. I went to hear a Welsh Preacher by the name of Maynard James. He had glory in his words, but it was not the power of rhetoric which gave me a longing to become part of the family of God. Someone said to me, at the close of the service, "If you become a Christian you will never be lonely again", and this was the word I needed to hear. So, I joined the chorus line, and I have had a song in my soul ever since. Christians belong to the greatest fellowship on earth. We belong to the family of God. Nothing can separate us from the love of God in Christ Jesus our lord.

The Huddersfield Choral Society became famous because of the clarity of its diction. This happened because most of its choristers worked in woollen mills and had learned to speak clearly above the noise of the looms. To sing in the heavenly choir, it is necessary to be able to speak above the clamour of society today and identify the language of heaven.

Hallelujah! Sing to Jesus

Words

I was surprised to find the same joke inside many of the crackers at Christmas! Numerous times I read, "Where do elves go when they are sick? To the elf (Health) centre, of course."

I heard another play on words when a mother who gave birth to twins on Boxing day was greeted by, "A Nappy New Year."

In his book Cider with Rosie, Laurie Lee recalls being disillusioned by his first day at school. "They said, sit here for the present, and they never gave me one," he explained.

Words do not change, but their meaning can be changed by the way we speak them, or by our own perception of their meaning. Consider this notice outside a community centre: "Members of Weight watchers, please use the double doors at the back of the building."

The Bible is the Word of God, and Jesus is described as the Word made flesh, dwelling among us. I am so grateful that Jesus began his ministry to present God to the world as a carpenter in Nazareth. Carpentry is a creative job. A carpenter works with care, using tools that could cut and bruise. He works with patience, using materials that might be hard, which might splinter and spoil, which can resist his greatest effort to turn them into something useful or beautiful.

In a busy work shop he would meet every type of person; he would encounter every human foible, fancy, feeling, fault. It was 30 years before Jesus was ready to present God to the kaleidoscopic population of planet Earth in a way that they would understand. The Carpenter of Nazareth took time to fully understand humanity. He continues to work with care and patience and his whole purpose is to create beauty and usefulness out of our original material.

St Paul gave this advice to a church in Philippi: *"Rejoice in the Lord, and again I say, rejoice."*

We can step into the New Year, knowing that nothing takes God by surprise and that his promise is, *"I will never leave you, or forsake you."*

That is a cracker of a promise, it is not a joke!

www.ingramcontent.com/pod-product-compliance
Lightning Source LLC
Chambersburg PA
CBHW061513040426
42450CB00008B/1595